Cambridge Early Years

Communication and Language
for English as a Second Language

Learner's Book 3A

Claire Medwell

Contents

Note to parents and practitioners   3

Block 1: Places near and far   4

Block 2: Farms and being outside   21

Acknowledgements   32

Note to parents and practitioners

This Learner's Book provides activities to support the first term of ESL Communication and Language for Cambridge Early Years 3.

Activities can be used at school or at home. Children will need support from an adult. Additional guidance about activities can be found in the **For practitioners** boxes.

Stories are provided for children to enjoy looking at and listening to. Children are not expected to be able to read the stories themselves.

Children will encounter the following characters within this book. You could ask children to point to the characters when they see them on the pages, and say their names.

The Learner's Book activities support the Teaching Resource activities. The Teaching Resource provides step-by-step coverage of the Cambridge Early Years curriculum and guidance on how the Learner's Book activities develop the curriculum learning statements.

Hi, my name is Mia.

Find us on the front covers doing lots of fun activities.

Hi, my name is Gemi.

Hi, my name is Rafi.

Hi, my name is Kiho.

Block 1 — Places near and far

What Is My Job? (Sung to the tune of *Frère Jacques*)

What is my job? What is my job?
Do you know? Do you know?
I teach you new things,
I teach you new things.
Who am I? Who am I? *(Teacher!)*

What is my job? What is my job?
Do you know? Do you know?
I care for animals,
I care for animals.
Who am I? Who am I? *(Vet!)*

What is my job? What is my job?
Do you know? Do you know?
I make you better,
I make you better.
Who am I? Who am I? *(Doctor!)*

What is my job? What is my job?
Do you know? Do you know?
I grow your food,
I grow your food.
Who am I? Who am I? *(Farmer!)*

In the school

Match.

Match the school helpers to the objects.

For practitioners
Invite children to identify the school helpers they can see in the pictures and to match them to the objects they use in their job.

What is my job?
Circle and say.

For practitioners
Children find and circle the people and their uniforms, and use as stimulus for talk. Encourage them to respond to simple questions by pointing to the correct picture, for example, *Where is the firefighter?* Encourage further talk using subject pronouns, e.g., *she is a dentist*.

The Umbrella Tree

One day, in the middle of nowhere,
a tiny green shoot begins to grow.

Each day it grows UP and UP towards the sun.
There is little water and there are no other trees.

Little leaves appear … 1, 2, 3, 4, 5!
Soon, the little shoot becomes a small tree!

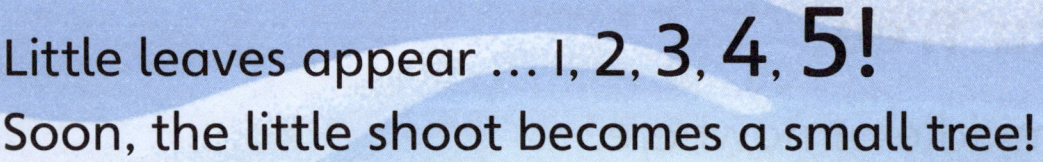

The summer is LONG and HOT, the wind blows through its branches. It moves from side to side.

Storms come with LIGHTNING BOLTS and THUNDER CLAPS … but still the tree grows! Its branches grow wide and full of green leaves.

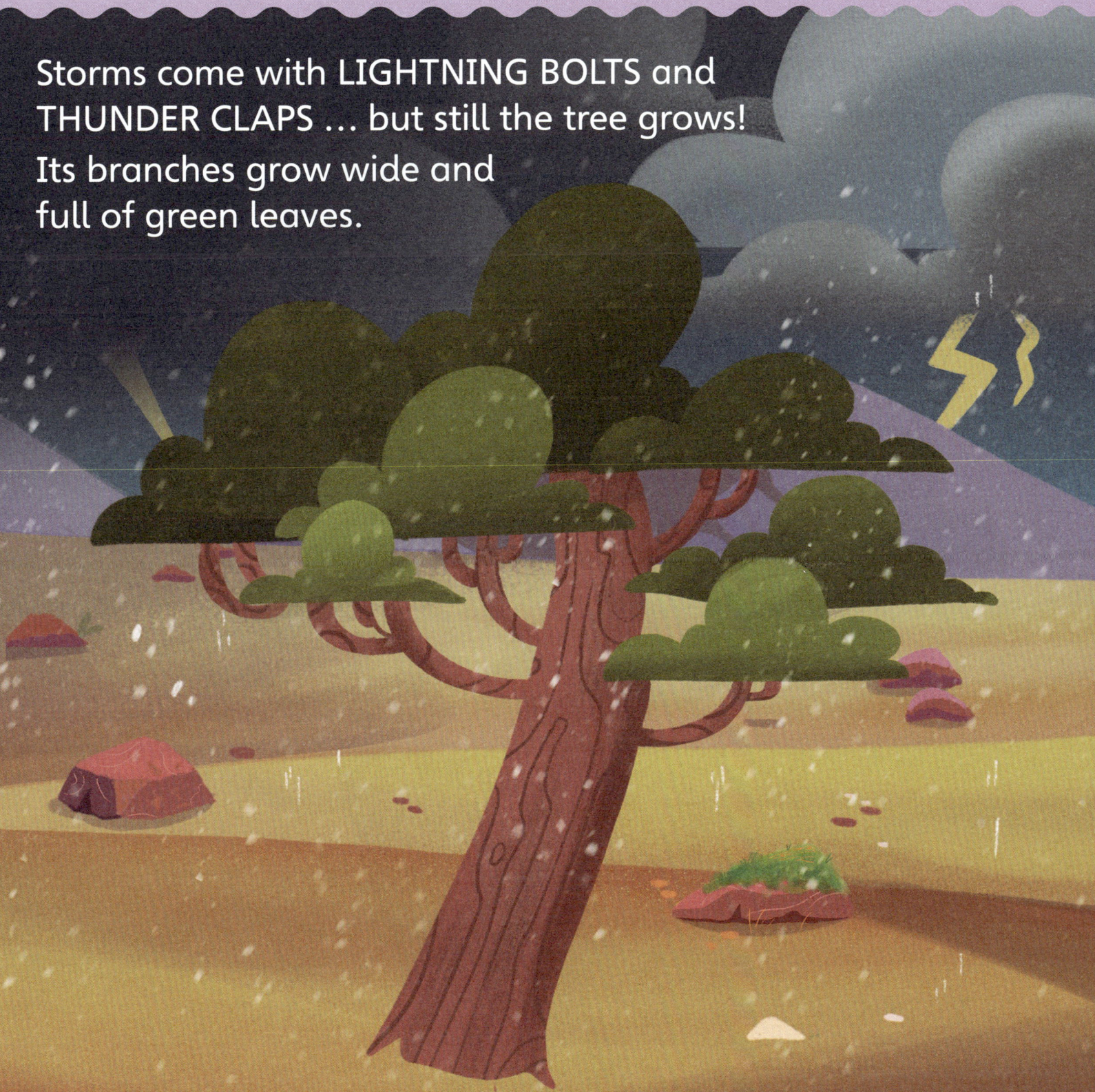

"*I'm so lonely,*" thought the umbrella tree.
One day, a little colourful roller bird flies up to the tree.

"What a BEAUTIFUL tree! Can I make my nest in your branches?"

"Yes, of course!" said the umbrella tree.

Soon after, the umbrella tree heard a voice nearby. "Hello! What a BEAUTIFUL tree! Can I live here?"

"*Who are you? I can't see you!*" said the umbrella tree.

"*Here I am!*" said the chameleon, changing its colour.

"*Of course you can live here!*" said the umbrella tree. "*I'm so happy!*"

As the tree GREW and GREW, more small animals came to rest under its branches.

One day, a family of meerkats with BIG, BLACK eyes and an aardvark with pointy ears came to visit.

The umbrella tree wasn't lonely anymore. The bigger it grew, the bigger the animals were which came to visit.

A spotty cheetah flashed up one day and surprised the umbrella tree.

"*Hey, what a BEAUTIFUL tree you are! Can I sleep here a while?*"

"*Yes, of course!*" said the surprised umbrella tree.

Another day a TALL, LONG-LEGGED giraffe passed by …

"What a BEAUTIFUL tree you are!" said the giraffe. "Can I eat some of your delicious leaves?"

The umbrella tree became a place for people to meet, to celebrate and for children to play!

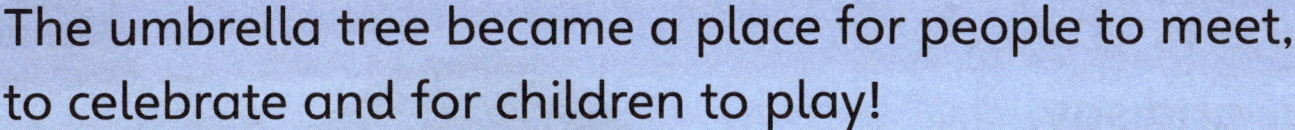

To this very day, its branches and leaves protect everyone from the hot sun, bringing comfort and peace to all!

The umbrella tree was never lonely again!

Where is the…?

Colour and say.

Find and name the animals from the story. Colour them in.

Sentence mix up!

Match and say.

Match the sentences to the pictures.

1. The tree is big and green.

2. There are four bird eggs.

3. It's eating leaves.

4. It's sleeping.

For practitioners

Encourage children to talk about what they can see in each picture before they match them to the sentences. Children can read the sentences aloud independently or with support.

My favourite animal

Think and draw.

Draw your favourite animal in the picture frame.

My favourite animal is _____ .

> **For practitioners**
> Ask children to think about and describe their favourite animal as they draw. For example, *It's brown and yellow. It's got two legs.* Children write the name of the animal on the line. Provide support if needed.

I like ...

Look and say.

Talk about what the children are doing.

For practitioners

Encourage talk about the activities children are doing in the picture. Remind them to use the pronouns *he*, *she*, *they*. Ask children which of the activities in the picture they like doing.

Block 2 Farms and being outside

Hickory Dickory Dock

Hickory, dickory, dock!
The mouse ran up the clock!
The clock struck one,
The mouse ran down.
Hickory, dickory, dock!

Tickory, dickory, doo!
The town hall clock struck two!
The King fell down,
And broke his crown.
Tickory, dickory, doo!

Tickery, dickory, dee!
The church bell clock struck three!
The nest fell down,
And all around,
Were beautiful birds to see!

Hickory, dickory, door!
The old school bell struck four!
They closed their books,
Put on their coats,
And all ran out the door!

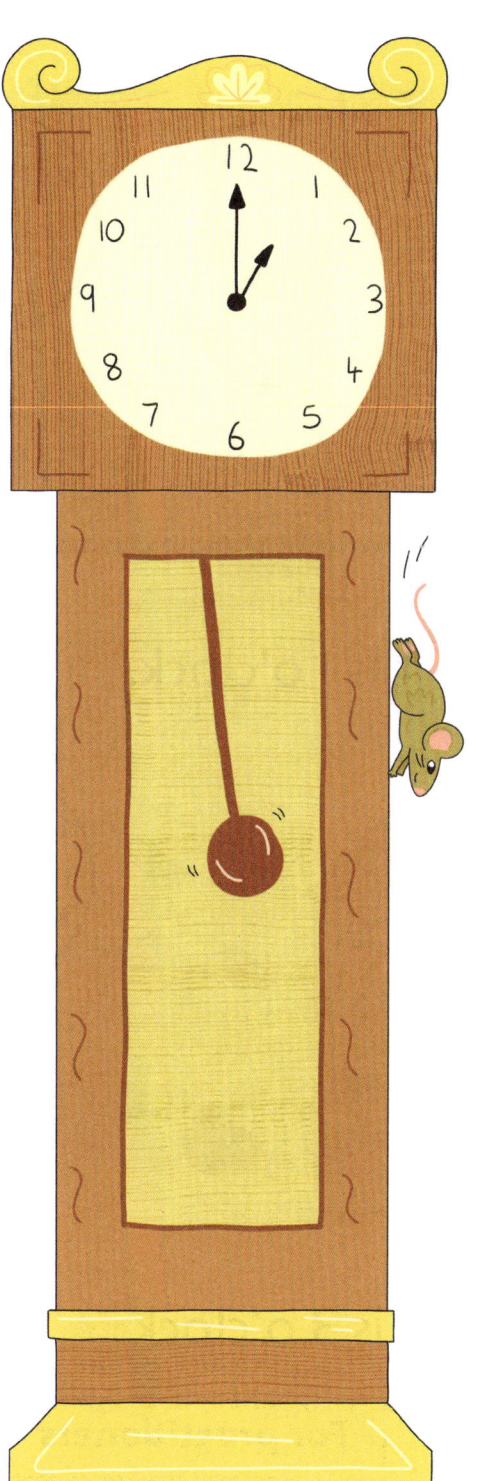

What's the time?

Read and say.

Say the time and talk about the pictures.

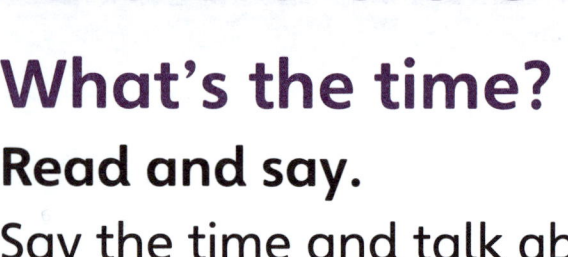

It is 1 o'clock.

It is 2 o'clock.

It is 3 o'clock.

It is 4 o'clock.

For practitioners

Children read the simple sentences. Provide help if required signalling each word as you read from left to right. Children point and follow. They then say the time showing on each clock. Talk about images from the rhyme to help support understanding of the context.

Recycling is Fun by Charles Ghigna

Recycling is a lot of fun,
for you and me and everyone!

Putting paper in its place puts a smile on your face!

Paper, plastic, glass, and tin …
We put each one into a bin.

Hurray! Hurray! Recycle day!
A big truck takes our trash away.

We clean out all our dresser drawers and donate clothes to Goodwill stores.

We save some buttons from the box and make hand puppets from old socks.

We cut old sleeves, and then we make each of our friends a big pet snake!

We help the planet when we choose to recycle and reuse!

Same or different?

Circle and say.

Circle the object which is a different material in each row. Say what it is made of.

For practitioners

Remind children of the materials they have been learning about: paper, glass, plastic and metal. Ask them to identify the material of each object. Point and ask *What's this?* and establish the one which is different in each row.

Let's recycle!

Match and say.

Name the objects.
Match them with the recycled items.

Look at my rocket! I made it from a cardboard tube!

For practitioners

Prior to the matching activity, encourage children to name the original objects and what say they are made from. Then ask children to think about new objects they could make from each one. If time, provide children with old materials ready for recycling. Ask them to make something new from them just like Rafi did.

My sock puppet

Draw and colour.

Look at the example.
Create and colour your sock puppet. Give it a name.

My name is Arthur.

My sock puppet is called _____.

For practitioners
Point to the sock puppet. Use simple words and phrases to describe it. Children repeat. They then draw and colour their own. Encourage children to talk about their puppets, e.g., *This is my puppet. Its name is …*

Put it in the bin!

Sort and say.

Find the correct bins for the objects. Draw the routes.

For practitioners

Monitor as children engage in the activity. Ask them to identify the material of each object. Respond by saying *Let's put the (paper tube) in the (paper) bin.*

I spy

Look and make.

Talk about the pictures.
Then make an *I spy* bottle.

For practitioners

Provide pre-made *I spy* bottles. Encourage children to explore and identify the items in the jar using simple words and phrases. Provide materials for them to make their own *I spy* bottles in pairs. Make a table display to encourage interaction and talk about their craft.

Acknowledgements

The authors and publishers acknowledge the following sources of copyright material and are grateful for the permissions granted. While every effort has been made, it has not always been possible to identify the sources of all the material used, or to trace all copyright holders. If any omissions are brought to our notice, we will be happy to include the appropriate acknowledgements on reprinting.

Recycling is Fun by Charles Ghigna, illustrated by Ag Jatcowska, Copyright © 2012 Picture Window Books. All rights reserved. Used with permission from Capstone Publishing, Mankato, Minnesota

Thanks to the following artists at Beehive Illustration:

Laura Arias, Lays Bittencourt, Tamara Joubert, John Lund, Michelle McGovern, Claire Philpott.

Cover characters by Becky Davies (The Bright Agency)